IT'S COOL TO LEARN ABOUT COUNTRIES

Social Studies Explorer

MEXICO

↠ by Barbara A. Somervill

CHERRY LAKE PUBLISHING • ANN ARBOR, MICHIGAN

Published in the United States of America
by Cherry Lake Publishing
Ann Arbor, Michigan
www.cherrylakepublishing.com

Content Adviser: Mauricio Tenorio-Trillo, PhD,
Department of History, University of Chicago

Book design: The Design Lab

Photo credits: Cover and page 1, ©Vivid Pixels/Shutterstock, Inc.; cover (stamp),
©iStockphoto.com/tomograf; page 4, ©Hannamariah/Shutterstock, Inc.; page 6,
©iStockphoto.com/2ndLookGraphics; page 9, ©Ivan Sgualdini/Shutterstock, Inc.; page
10, ©Mike Liu/Shutterstock, Inc.; page 11, ©Danilo Ascione/Shutterstock, Inc.; pages
13 and 16, ©Keith Dannemiller/Alamy; page 18, ©Feverpitch/Shutterstock, Inc.;
page 19, ©Ales Liska/Shutterstock, Inc.; page 21, ©The Art Archive/Alamy; page 23,
©Jon Arnold Images Ltd/Alamy; page 25, ©Dalayo/Dreamstime.com; page 26, ©Bobby
Deal/RealDealPhoto/Shutterstock, Inc.; page 27, ©iStockphoto.com/Coast-to-Coast;
page 32, ©Image Source/Alamy; page 33, ©iStockphoto.com/Alija; page 36, ©wendy
connett/Alamy; page 37, ©Kim Karpeles/Alamy; page 38, ©B.G. Smith/Shutterstock,
Inc.; page 41, ©iStockphoto.com/travellinglight; page 42, ©Evok20/Shutterstock, Inc.;
page 43, ©Karin Hildebrand Lau/Shutterstock, Inc.; page 44, ©tacar/Shutterstock, Inc.

Library of Congress Cataloging-in-Publication Data
Somervill, Barbara A.
    It's cool to learn about countries: Mexico/by Barbara A. Somervill.
        p. cm.—(Social studies explorer)
    Includes bibliographical references and index.
    ISBN-13: 978-1-60279-833-5 (lib. bdg.)
    ISBN-10: 1-60279-833-8 (lib. bdg.)
1. Mexico—Juvenile literature. I. Title. II. Title: Mexico. III. Series.
    F1208.5.S64 2011
    972—dc22   2010005508

Cherry Lake Publishing would like to acknowledge the work of The Partnership for
21st Century Skills. Please visit www.21stcenturyskills.org for more information.

Printed in the United States of America
Corporate Graphics Inc.
August 2011
CLFA07

TABLE OF CONTENTS

CHAPTER ONE

¡BIENVENIDOS A MÉJICO!

☞ Chichén Itzá attracts tourists from around the world.

Welcome to Mexico! Lace up your hiking boots. We'll need them as we trek to the top of an ancient Mayan pyramid at Chichén Itzá. Next, let's tromp through a dense rainforest on the lookout for brightly colored parrots and macaws. When we head north, the colors of the land will change from lush greens to the soft reds and browns of the Sonoran desert. We'll also shop in an open market.

Mexico's official name is Estados Unidos Mexicanos, or the United Mexican States. To the north lays the United States of America. To the south are Belize and Guatemala. The Gulf of Mexico and the Caribbean Sea lap Mexico's eastern shores. To the west are more beaches, the Pacific Ocean, and the Gulf of California.

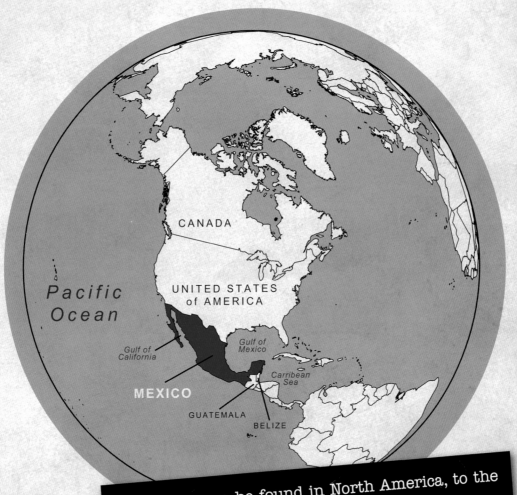

➺ Mexico can be found in North America, to the south of the United States of America.

Mexico is the fifteenth-largest country in the world. Its total area is 758,449 square miles (1,964,375 square kilometers). That is approximately three times the size of Texas. Mexico's land features rugged, volcanic mountains and broad **plateaus**. This nation is also home to steamy tropical jungles and bone-dry deserts. The Sierra Madre Oriental mountain range runs along the eastern side of the country. The Sierra Madre Occidental and the Sierra Madre del Sur run down the west. Between the ranges is a high plateau called the Mexican *altiplano*, or high plain. It is also referred to as the central plain.

➥ Many Mexicans make their homes in the country's mountain ranges.

Mexico is bordered to the east and west by large bodies of water. Using a separate sheet of paper, trace the map of Mexico. Include these bodies of water on your map: the Pacific Ocean, the Gulf of California, the Gulf of Mexico, and the Caribbean Sea. Mexico also has two major peninsulas. A peninsula is a piece of land that extends out from a larger landmass into a body of water. Be sure to label Baja California and the Yucatán Peninsula. Which bodies of water border Baja California? Which bodies of water touch the Yucatán?

Mexico has many rivers and a handful of large lakes. Fresh water is a major environmental issue in Mexico. Mexico City, the country's capital, is sinking. Why? The city was constructed on a lake bed that is not very stable. There are reserves of water in the rock beneath the city. As that water is drained and used up, the city sinks. At one time, the *altiplano* was filled with lakes and wetlands. After 500 years of draining lakes and filling wetlands, that water source is nearly dried up. Drought, high rates of water usage by Mexico's people, and pollution have reduced the supply of clean water even further.

In 2007, divers found what may be the longest underground river in the world on the Yucatán Peninsula. The river winds along a 95-mile (153 kilometer) stretch through a series of limestone caves. The water flows in two layers. There is a thin layer of fresh water on top of a layer of salt water.

MEXICO

20¢ 1977-78

Having fresh water supplies is only one environmental concern for Mexico. Clearing forestland for building has led to widespread **erosion**. In the north, the deserts are spreading. As the country became more industrial, problems with pollution also increased.

Mexico has one of the greatest levels of **biodiversity** on Earth. It is home to more than 500 species of mammals. The country has many critically **endangered** rat, bat, and mouse species. Its waters are home to endangered blue whales, fin whales, and sea otters. Rapid growth and environmental problems have had a negative impact on the country's wildlife. Fortunately, a number of organizations work to protect Mexico's wildlife.

The toucan is one of the many kinds of birds that can be found in Mexico.

CHAPTER TWO

BUSINESS AND GOVERNMENT IN MEXICO

→ Resort cities like Cancun are the driving
force behind Mexico's tourism industry.

Mexicans work in many different kinds of jobs. Approximately 15 percent of workers have jobs related to agriculture. Nearly 26 percent work in jobs related to manufacturing goods. The majority of Mexico's 45 million workers—59 percent—earn money by providing services.

People with careers in service industries do not produce goods for sale. Instead, they sell their time, effort, and ideas. A major service industry in Mexico is tourism. The tourism industry includes travel agents, taxi drivers, and hotel and restaurant workers. Musicians and dancers are also service providers. So are park rangers and police officers.

The main currency of Mexico is the peso. In 2010, one U.S. dollar equaled approximately 12.7 Mexican pesos. There are coins in the amounts of 1, 2, 5, 10, and 20 pesos. The country prints bills for 20, 50, 100, 200, and 500 pesos. A peso is made up of 100 centavos. Centavo coins come in amounts of 5, 10, 20, and 50 centavos.

Farm products account for less than 4 percent of Mexico's **gross domestic product**. Corn is a staple food for all Mexicans. It is the most important crop that is grown. Mexico also produces wheat, soybeans, rice, and beans. Coffee, fruit, tomatoes, beef, and poultry are produced, too. Mexico **exports** some fruits, vegetables, and grain to other countries.

Do you want to know more about Mexico's economy? Take a look at its trading partners. Trading partners are the countries that **import** goods from a country or export goods to that country. Here is a graph showing the countries that are Mexico's top import and export trading partners.

EXPORTS ← MEXICO ← IMPORTS

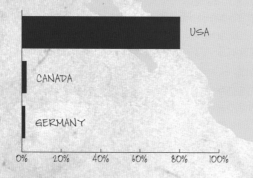

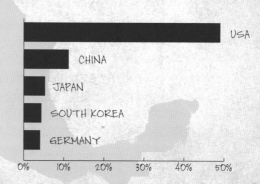

◆ Maquiladoras employ many Mexican workers.

Mexico exports approximately $200 billion dollars of products to the United States each year. A key part of Mexico's economy is the *maquiladora*. Maquiladoras are factories that are owned by non-Mexican companies. Raw materials or parts are brought into Mexico to be turned into products at the maquiladoras. These products are then shipped for sale elsewhere. Many maquiladoras can be found in cities bordering the United States, including Tijuana, Juárez, and Mexicali. Clothing, cars, and electronic equipment are assembled at maquiladoras. The advantage for foreign investors is clear. Mexican wage and benefit costs are low. At the same time, the number and quality of available workers is high.

ACTIVITY

Put your graphing skills to the test. Make a bar graph showing the percentages of Mexico's labor force. One bar will represent those who work in agriculture. Another bar will represent people with jobs related to manufacturing. The third bar will represent workers who provide services. Use the percentages found at the beginning of this chapter. Ask an adult for help if you need it. Which bar will be the longest? Which will be the shortest?

Mexico's federal and state governments encourage foreign investors to build factories, hotels, and restaurants in the country. Investors get tax breaks. They also provide wages that support the country's economy.

Mexico's government is much like the government in the United States. An elected president guides the country with the help of a cabinet of advisors. Presidents are elected for one 6-year term. In 2006, Felipe Calderón Hinojosa became Mexico's president.

NAFTA stands for North American Free Trade Agreement. It is an economic agreement between the United States, Mexico, and Canada. Signed in 1994, NAFTA gets rid of most tariffs, or taxes, on goods traded among the members. Goods that are traded include food crops, clothing, cars, and electronics.

The legislative branch of government is the *Congreso de la Unión*, or the Congress of the Union. There are two houses of Congress. In the Senate, 96 members are elected by popular vote. They serve 6-year terms. Members of political parties fill another 32 seats. Parties get some of the 32 seats depending on the percentage of the vote they earned. Mexico has several major political parties. The three main parties are the Partido Acción Nacional (PAN), the Partido Revolucionario Institucional (PRI), and the Partido de la Revolución Democrática (PRD).

As president, Felipe Calderón works with the Congress of the Union to create new laws.

The Mexican flag is divided into three equal sections of green, white, and red. Nearly two centuries ago, its colors were selected to represent important ideas from Mexico's struggle for independence from Spain. The green represented hope for a better nation. White represented the Catholic faith. Red represented blood, which honors the country's heroes. The country's seal is in the center of the white section.

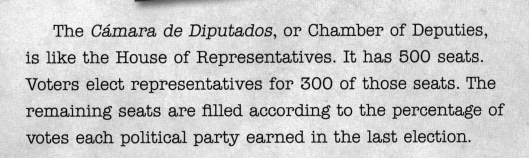

The *Cámara de Diputados*, or Chamber of Deputies, is like the House of Representatives. It has 500 seats. Voters elect representatives for 300 of those seats. The remaining seats are filled according to the percentage of votes each political party earned in the last election.

CHAPTER THREE

THE PEOPLE OF MEXICO

→ The people of Mexico share a rich cultural history.

Mexican culture traces its heritage back to ancient peoples. Many years ago, Mexico was home to the Mayas, the Mexica (me-SHEE-ka), and the Aztecs.

The Mayas lived on the Yucatán Peninsula and in Central America. Mayan religious ceremonies took place at pyramids. Some of these pyramids have survived to this day. The pyramids at Chichén Itzá, Palenque, and Tulum stretched high above the jungle. Mayans traveling from one community to another used the pyramids as landmarks on their trips.

→ Ruins of ancient pyramids have helped us learn a lot about Mayan culture and history.

The name *Mexico* comes from the Mexica, a group that settled in the area that is now Mexico City. This region is located between two major mountain ranges. It also became home to the Aztec culture. The Aztec economy was based on agriculture and war. Its main crop was corn. Today, corn remains a major crop for Mexico's people.

Tenochtitlán was the capital city of the Aztecs. According to legend, the site for this beautiful city was chosen in response to a sign from the gods. The Aztecs saw an eagle atop a cactus with a serpent in its mouth on an island in Lake Texcoco. They believed this was a sign telling them to settle there. The Spanish eventually built what would become Mexico City on top of this amazing Aztec city

MEXICO

20¢ 1977·78

⚬ Cortés and his soldiers began the era
of Spanish colonialism in Mexico.

From 1519 to 1521, Hernán Cortés and the Spanish
invaded the land. With the help of powerful local groups,
they conquered the Aztecs and other native peoples.
This conquest, along with centuries of colonial rule,
would forever change the land and the people who lived
there. What would eventually become Mexico emerged

from those centuries of huge changes. The impact of the Spanish on the region survives to this day. Spanish is the language of the Mexican people. The Roman Catholic faith, brought by the Spanish, is practiced by approximately 90 percent of residents. Sixty percent of people in Mexico are *mestizo*. Mestizos are people of mixed European and native ethnicity.

STOP Don't write in this book!

Imagine that you are at an open market in Mexico. All the signs are in Spanish. Can you figure out what is on sale today? On a separate sheet of paper, match the Spanish words with their English translations. See below for the answers.

Spanish	English
1. tomates [toh-MAH-tess]	a. books
2. pantalones [pahn-tah-LOH-ness]	b. bread
3. limón [lee-MOHN]	c. tomatoes
4. libros [LEE-brohss]	d. lemon
5. zapatos [sah-PAH-tohss]	e. dishes
6. pan [PAHN]	f. shoes
7. platos [PLAH-tohss]	g. pants

Answers: 1-c; 2-g; 3-d; 4-a; 5-f; 6-b; 7-e

➤ Many Mayan people preserve the traditions of their ancestors.

As of 2009, Mexico's population was estimated to be 111,211,789 people. The population is growing at a rate of slightly more than 1 percent yearly.

Mexico has several ethnic groups, most of which have native ties. The largest group is the Nahua, who are related to the Aztecs. More than 1.7 million Mexicans speak Nahuatl. There are also 1 million or more Maya speakers. Mexico is also home to populations of Zapotecs, Mixtecs, and Totonacs.

More than three-fourths of Mexico's population lives in cities. Mexicans shop in modern malls and supermarkets. There are also open markets. Here, smart buyers can get good deals on fresh fruits, pottery, and other goods.

Do you live in the United States? If so, there is a good chance that you have classmates or friends with cultural ties to Mexico. You may even be Mexican or Mexican American yourself. It would take another book to cover the rich history and experiences that strongly link Mexico to its northern neighbor. Would you like to learn more about the cultural and historical ties these countries share? Try some independent research. Ask a librarian to help you find books and other resources on these topics.

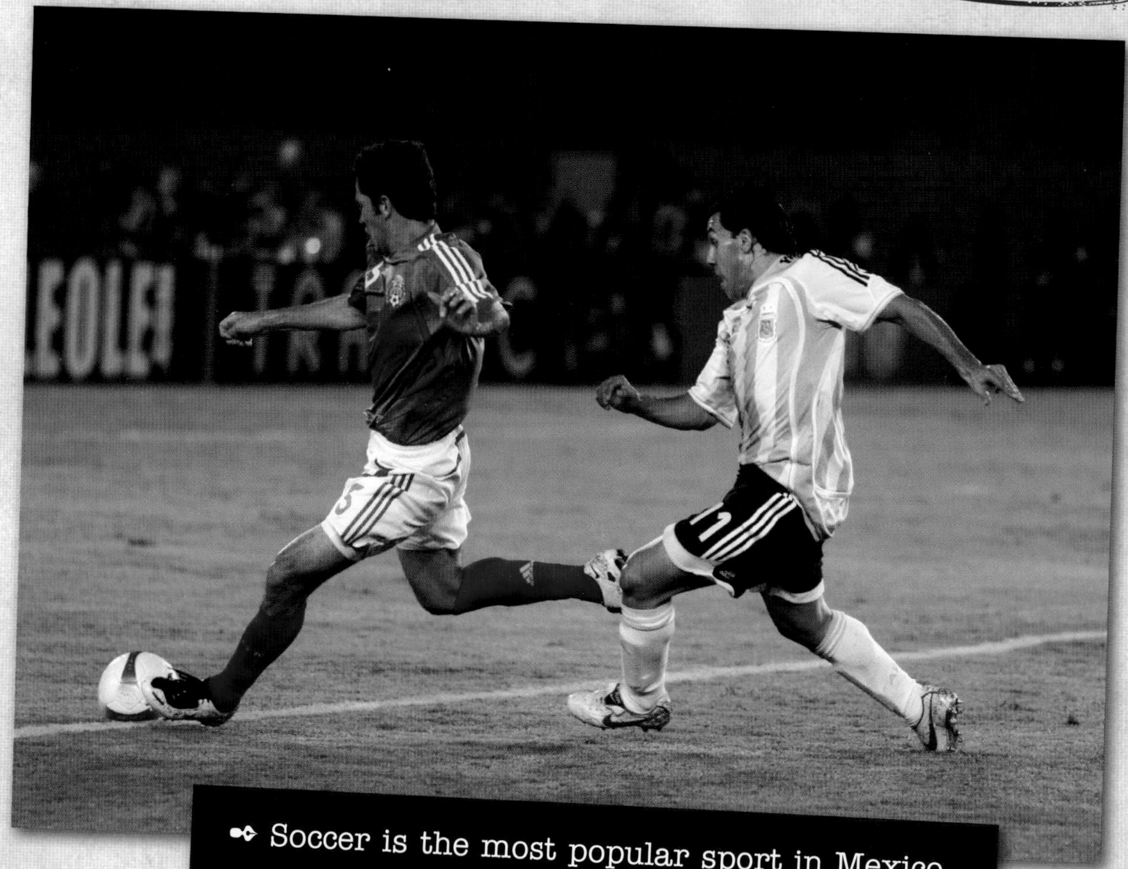

Soccer is the most popular sport in Mexico.

For entertainment, Mexicans listen to music, watch television, and follow their favorite soccer teams. Television shows include U.S. programs in Spanish, sporting events, and *telenovelas*. A telenovela is a type of **soap opera**. Mexicans love *fútbol*. You may know this sport as soccer. Victories are often followed by celebrations. Let's learn more about how Mexicans like to celebrate.

CHAPTER FOUR

¡FIESTAS!

➽ Día de los Muertos is often celebrated with parades and costumes.

Fiestas [fee-ESS-tahss], or parties and celebrations, in Mexico can revolve around life events. Birthdays and weddings are two examples. They can also be religious holidays, such as *Día de los Santos Reyes*, the *Semana Santa*, or *Día de los Muertos*. Some fiestas are national holidays.

In Mexico, people celebrate two "birthdays." The first is the anniversary of one's birth. The second falls on one's name day or saint's day. Children are usually named for a Roman Catholic saint. Each saint has a saint's day. A boy named Francisco, for example, would celebrate on the Feast of St. Francis, which is October 4. Mexican birthday parties feature great food, singing, and *piñatas* [peen-YAH-tahss] loaded with goodies.

↪ Piñatas come in many different shapes, colors, and sizes.

Piñatas are decorated containers filled with small gifts and treats. Let's make a pig piñata. You will need to use a stove to heat some of your materials and a knife for cutting. Be sure to ask an adult for help.

MATERIALS

- 1 large balloon
- Sheets of newspaper
- Approximately 50 2-inch (5.1 centimeters) squares of pink crepe paper
- Black marker pen
- 1 cup (237 milliliters) flour
- 2 cups (473 ml) water
- 6 3-ounce (85 grams) paper cups
- Tape
- Glue stick
- 1 pink pipe cleaner
- Saucepan
- Whisk
- Stove
- Serrated knife
- Paintbrush
- Nontoxic pink paint
- Scissors

1. Combine the water and flour in a saucepan to form a paste. Whisk the mixture to remove any lumps.
2. Have an adult heat the paste on the stove until thick. Allow the paste to cool.
3. Cover your work area with newspaper. Blow up the balloon and tie off the neck. The balloon is the pig's body.
4. Tape 4 cups to the balloon where the legs of a pig would go. Tape a cup over the knot you tied in the balloon's neck. This is the snout. Create 2 ears by cutting the last cup in half from top to bottom using scissors. Tape the ears to the top of the pig's head.

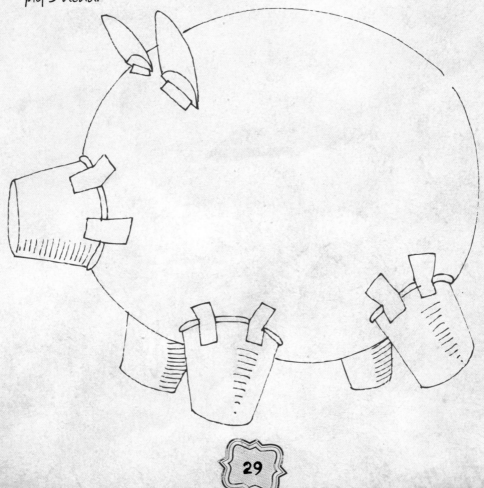

5. Cut the newspaper into strips that are 1.5 inches (3.8 cm) wide. Coat the strips with your paste and wrap them around the balloon, one at a time. Cover the entireballoon. Cover the the legs and snout, too. Repeat this process until you have placed 4 layers of strips on the pig. Allow the pig to dry for at least 2 days.

6. Wind the pipe cleaner into a spiral. Tape one end of the pipe cleaner to the piñata where a pig's tail would go.

7. Have an adult carefully cut a rectangular flap into the underside of the pig's belly using a serrated knife. Fold the flap back and pop the balloon.

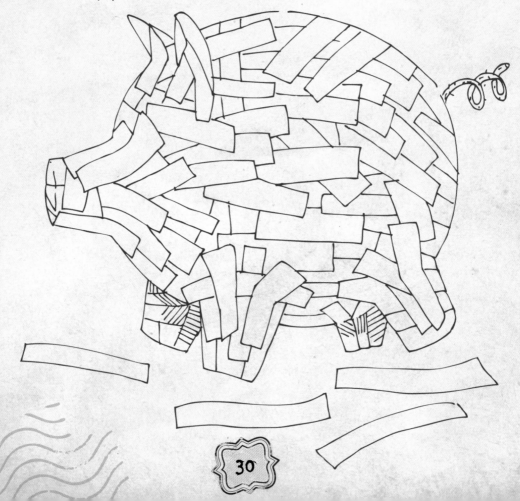

8. Fill the piñata with candy. Tape the flap closed.

9. Use a paintbrush to paint the entire pig with a layer of pink paint. Allow the paint to dry.

10. Use a glue stick to attach the pink squares to the pig. Overlap the squares to completely cover the piñata.

11. With a marker, draw eyes, nostrils, and a mouth on your pig.

Now comes the fun part. Whack the piñata and get the candy!

Girls celebrate a special birthday when they turn 15. This celebration is the *quinceañera* [keen-say-ahn-YER-ah]. This event begins with a Catholic mass honoring the girl. She wears a long gown and a tiara and carries flowers. Parents invite family and friends for a big party. The girl asks her closest friends to be part of her court of honor.

➧ Many Mexican families spare no expense when it comes time to plan a quinceañera celebration.

❧ Mexican celebrations often feature mariachi music.

Weddings are festive occasions. Bridesmaids and groomsmen work in pairs to provide the happy couple with a great day. One pair brings the bride's flowers. Another gives her the *Lazo*, a special rosary. After the wedding mass at church, a huge reception is held.

HOLIDAYS

These are some public holidays that are recognized in Mexico:

January 1	New Year's Day
February 5	Constitution Day
March 21	Birthday of Benito Juárez
May 1	Labor Day
May 5	Anniversary of the Battle of Puebla
September 16	Independence Day
October 12	Día de la Raza
November 1 and 2	Día de los Muertos
November 20	Revolution Day
December 12	Day of Our Lady of Guadalupe
December 25	Christmas Day

Because most Mexicans are Catholic, the country celebrates Catholic holidays. January 6 is Día de los Santos Reyes, or Day of the Holy Kings. This day celebrates the belief that three kings brought gifts to the baby Jesus Christ.

Religion plays an important role in the lives of many Mexicans. Even so, the government is **secular**. There is a strict separation between state and religious matters.

Carnaval takes place just before Lent. There are parades, floats, and dancing in the streets. Lent follows with 40 days of sacrifice and prayer, leading up to the Semana Santa, or Holy Week. On Easter, Mexicans break eggs filled with confetti over the heads of friends and family.

→ Families leave out food for the spirits of their dead relatives on Día de los Muertos.

Día de los Muertos, or Day of the Dead, blends Catholic All Saints' Day ceremonies with the Aztec tradition of honoring the dead. Elements from All Souls' Day are also incorporated. Día de los Muertos is held on November 1 and 2. It is a time for families to make altars to welcome the spirits of dead family members home. Special foods are served. Some include candy in the shape of skulls, candied pumpkin, and *pan de muertos*, or bread of the dead.

Mexico also has national holidays that celebrate key days in the nation's history. February 5 is Constitution Day, followed on February 21 by Flag Day. *Cinco de Mayo* celebrates the Mexican victory over the French army at Puebla in 1862. Mexican Independence Day is held on September 16.

◆➤ Mexicans show pride for their country with parades and parties on Independence Day.

CHAPTER FIVE

WHAT'S ON THE MENU?

➛ A tostada is a crispy tortilla topped with meat, vegetables, and salsa.

They're thin. They're round. They're used in many Mexican dishes. Have you guessed what they are yet? Tortillas! These Mexican flatbreads can be made of corn or wheat flour. They can be filled with cheese, meat, tomatoes, lettuce, onions, and salsa. Tortillas are a basic ingredient of tacos, enchiladas, flautas, and burritos. In Mexico, tortillas are served at many meals.

Want to taste a snack that many Mexican kids enjoy? Try this simple recipe that serves 4. Ask an adult to help you with any slicing or chopping.

Cucumbers with Lime and Chile

INGREDIENTS
4 small cucumbers
4 limes
1 tablespoon (14.8 ml) salt
chile powder (to taste)

Instructions are continued on the following page ⟶

INSTRUCTIONS

1. Store the cucumbers in the refrigerator until chilled. Have an adult use a knife to carefully cut the cucumbers into thin slices.

2. Place the cucumber slices in a bowl.

3. Squeeze the limes over the slices in the bowl.

4. Sprinkle the cucumber slices with the salt and chile powder.

5. Using tongs, mix the cucumbers, lime juice, salt, and chile powder.

6. Allow the cucumbers to sit for 5 minutes.

7. Put the cucumbers on plates. If you like, you can add another light sprinkling of salt and chile powder before serving. Enjoy!

Bright, bold flavors such as the ones found in this dish are a common characteristic of many Mexican foods. Next time, try replacing the cucumbers in this recipe with carrots or a root called jicama. Then share this Mexican street snack with friends and family.

➥ Huevos rancheros are a great way to start the day.

Breakfast in Mexico may consist of beans, rice and fried tortillas. People may also eat *huevos rancheros*. This dish features eggs with salsa and tortillas on the side. Coffee rounds out the meal. Many Mexicans like breakfast pastries, and children enjoy breakfast cereals.

Lunch and dinner include dishes containing beef, chicken, or pork along with refried beans, rice, tomatoes, and lettuce. Along the coasts, fish and shrimp may replace beef and chicken in meals.

☛ Mole is usually served with chicken.

➤ Peppers taste great and add a
dash of bright color to a meal.

Peppers add spice to any dish. Mexicans use very
mild ancho peppers in *chiles rellenos*, or stuffed chilies.
Other dishes may incorporate scorching-hot habaneros.
Peppers are an important ingredient in chili sauce. This
sauce is used to season many Mexican meals. For special meals, Mexicans may create a sauce called mole
(MOH-lay), made with unsweetened chocolate and other
ingredients.

When it is time for desert, there are many options. Fruit, cakes, and flan are a few choices. Flan is a type of custard. Vanilla, like certain cacao trees, is native to Mexico. It is a flavoring for many Mexican cookies. Coconut is also a popular addition to cookies and candy.

•❖ Flan is often topped with fresh fruit.

Hot chocolate is a favorite treat for many Mexicans, just as it was for the Aztecs. The Aztecs, however, did not drink chocolate with sugar, but with ground hot peppers.

Have your travels left you wanting more? Your exploration of Mexico doesn't have to stop here. Which cultural treasures will you uncover next?

GLOSSARY

biodiversity (bye-oh-dih-VURS-it-ee) the variety of different plants and animals living in a certain area

drought (DROUT) a long period of very dry weather

endangered (en-DAYN-jurd) at risk of dying out completely

environmental (en-vye-ruhn-MENT-uhl) having to do with the water, minerals, air, organisms, and other natural factors of an area

erosion (ih-ROH-zhuhn) a gradual wearing away of something by wind, water, or glaciers

exports (EK-sportss) sends something to another country to be sold there

gross domestic product (GROHSS doh-MESS-tik PROD-uhkt) the total value of goods produced and services provided in a country during one year

import (IM-port) bring in from another country

plateaus (pla-TOHZ) areas of high, flat land

secular (SEK-yuh-lur) not related to religion

soap opera (SOPE OP-ur-uh) a television series that is overly dramatic and emotional

FOR MORE INFORMATION

Books

Kalman, Bobbie. *Mexico: The Culture*. New York: Crabtree Publishing Company, 2009.

Landau, Elaine. *Mexico*. New York: Children's Press, 2008.

McDaniel, Jan. *The Food of Mexico*. Philadelphia: Mason Crest Publishers, 2009.

Web Sites

Central Intelligence Agency—The World Factbook: Mexico
www.cia.gov/library/publications/the-world-factbook/ geos/mx.html
This is a great resource for information about Mexico's economy, government, and more.

National Geographic Kids—Mexico
kids.nationalgeographic.com/Places/Find/Mexico
Read all about Mexico and check out beautiful photos at this site.

TIME for Kids—Mexico
www.timeforkids.com/TFK/kids/hh/goplaces/ main/0,28375,591663,00.html
Take a virtual tour of Mexico and find many facts at this informative site.

INDEX

ABOUT THE AUTHOR
Barbara Somervill has been to Mexico many times. She loves the food, the people, and the beautiful beaches. She learned to speak Spanish as a child and enjoys the opportunity to practice when she visits her favorite Mexican city, Puerto Vallarta.